HOLIDAYS, FESTIVALS, & CELEBRATIONS

DÍA DE LOS MUERTOS

BY ANN HEINRICHS · ILLUSTRATED BY MERNIE GALLAGHER-COLE

Published in the United States of America by The Child's World®
PO Box 326 • Chanhassen, MN 55317-0326
800-599-READ • www.childsworld.com

ACKNOWLEDGMENTS
The Child's World®: Mary Berendes, Publishing Director

Editorial Directions, Inc.: E. Russell Primm, Editorial Director; Katie Marsico, Managing Editor; Judith Shiffer,
Assistant Editor; Caroline Wood and Rory Mabin, Editorial Assistants; Susan Hindman, Copy Editor and
Proofreader; Elizabeth Nellums, Rory Mabin, Ruth Martin, and Caroline Wood, Fact Checkers; Tim Griffin/
IndexServ, Indexer

The Design Lab: Kathleen Petelinsek, Design and Page Production

LIBRARY OF CONGRESS CATALOGING-IN-PUBLICATION DATA
Heinrichs, Ann.
  Día de los muertos / by Ann Heinrichs ; illustrated by Mernie Gallagher-Cole.
    p. cm. — (Holidays, festivals, & celebrations)
  Includes index.
  ISBN 1-59296-574-1 (library bound : alk. paper)
  1. All Souls' Day—Juvenile literature. 2. Mexico—Social life and customs—Juvenile literature. I. Gallagher-Cole,
Mernie, ill. II. Title. III. Series.
  GT4995.A4H45 2006
  394.266—dc22   2005025679

TABLE OF CONTENTS

CHAPTER ONE

THE DAY OF THE DEAD

Skeletons dance in the windows. Children eat candy shaped like skulls. Tables are heaped with flowers and food. It's Día de los Muertos (DEE-ah day lohs MWEHR-tohs)!

Día de los Muertos is Spanish for "day of the dead." But it's not a sad holiday. It's full of joy! It's a time to celebrate loved ones who have died.

Día de los Muertos is a joyous festival!

People in Mexico celebrate *Día de los Muertos*. So do people in other parts of Central America and South America. Mexican Americans celebrate this holiday, too.

CHAPTER TWO

HOW IT ALL BEGAN

Aztec people once lived in Mexico. They held a festival to celebrate the dead. It lasted a whole month.

The Aztecs believed the spirits of the dead returned at this time. People rejoiced that their loved ones were visiting. They celebrated and danced. Skulls were part of the festival, too. They were **symbols** of death and rebirth.

Spanish people arrived in the 1500s. They were shocked at this festival. Spaniards saw death as the end of life. It was a time to be **grim.**

But the Aztecs had a different view. To them, death was part of the **cycle** of life. They watched this cycle every year. Their crops sprouted, grew, ripened, and died. Then the cycle began again.

The Aztecs' festival celebrated the cycle of life.

The Aztecs honored the goddess Mictecacihuatl (meek-tay-kah-SEE-hwahtl) at their festival of the dead. She was called the Lady of the Dead. The Aztecs believed she ruled the underworld.

THE FESTIVAL THAT LIVED ON

T he Spaniards were Christians. They taught their religion to the Aztecs. But they could not change the Aztecs' celebration of the dead. Instead, they joined it with Christian beliefs.

November 2 is All Souls' Day. This Christian feast honors the dead. Among the people of Mexico, it became Día de los Muertos.

The Aztecs' old beliefs did not die. People still believed the spirits visited on Día de los Muertos. And the living still rejoiced!

Spaniards taught Christianity to the Aztecs, Mayans, and many other people from Mexico, Central America, and South America.

The Aztecs and Spaniards combined their beliefs to create Día de los Muertos.

CHAPTER FOUR

THREE DAYS OF CELEBRATION

Día de los Muertos became a three-day festival. People begin celebrating on October 31, or Halloween. November 1 is the Christian feast of All Saints' Day. November 2 is All Souls' Day. These last two days are the main part of the Día de los Muertos celebration.

Día de los Muertos is very different from Halloween. Halloween treats death as scary. But Día de los Muertos is a happy time. It celebrates a loved one's life. And it laughs at death!

Día de los Muertos is a three-day festival.

Children who have died are called angelitos *(ahn-heh-LEE-tohs). That's Spanish for "little angels." Their spirits are believed to return on November 1.*

CHAPTER FIVE

VISITING GRAVES

On Día de los Muertos, people believe that the spirits of the dead return. The spirits visit with family members and friends who are still alive.

People who have lost loved ones look forward to Día de los Muertos. They believe the spirits of their dead family and friends return to visit.

Yellow marigolds are known as the flowers of the dead. They have a strong, sweet smell. That helps the spirits find their way home.

This is a time to visit a loved one's grave. People clean and repaint the gravestone. They place marigolds and other flowers around it. Candles are lit around the grave, too.

People often visit a loved one's grave during Día de los Muertos.

Friends and family members gather there.
They tell stories about the person. They laugh and
remember happy times. Often they have a picnic
around the grave. They pray for their loved one, too.
People may stay by the grave all through the night.

*People sometimes gather for a picnic during Día de los Muertos.
It is not unusual for this picnic to be at a loved one's grave.*

CHAPTER SIX

ALTARS AND OFFERINGS

People prepare their homes for Día de los Muertos. They set up **altars** to the dead. The altar welcomes the loved one home.

Photos of the person are placed on the altar. The photos show the people as they were when they were young and happy. Candles and flowers adorn the altar. Incense is burned there, too.

Many *ofrendas* (oh-FREHN-dahs), or offerings, are placed on the altar. They help the spirit find its way home. Ofrendas might include the person's favorite objects. If the person was a child, there are toys. Favorite foods are set out. So are bread and skull-shaped candy.

Ofrendas help a loved one's spirit find its way home.

The altar itself is sometimes called the ofrenda.

Mole (MOH-lay) and
tamales (tah-MAH-lays)
are often placed on the altar.
Mole is a thick, spicy sauce.
Tamales are meat or beans
wrapped in corn husks.

Colorful paper is hung above the altar. It's called *papel picado* (pah-PELL pee-KAH-doh). The paper is cut in pretty designs.

Papel picado decorates Día de los Muertos altars.

CHAPTER SEVEN

HAPPY SKELETONS

Skeletons are everywhere during Día de los Muertos. They are called *calacas* (kah-LAH-kahs).

Skeleton pictures are favorite decorations. What are the skeletons doing? Having fun! They are laughing or dancing. Some wear fancy clothes and jewelry. Huge, flowered hats sit atop their heads.

Skeleton figures are placed on altars. They're funny and playful. They may be relaxing in a chair or playing games. Or they might be working at what was once the dead person's job.

Día de los Muertos often includes a skeleton dance. People put on skull masks. Then they dance around gaily. It's a way of laughing at death!

Calacas figures are sometimes called calaveras *(kah-lah-VEH-rahs).*

People often celebrate Día de los Muertos with a skeleton dance.

CALAVERAS POEM

Spanish:

Ahí viene el agua
Por la ladera,
Y se me moja
Mi calavera.

La muerte calaca,
Ni gorda ni flaca.
La muerte casera,
Pegada con cera.

CALAVERAS POEM

English:

Here comes the water
Down the slope
And my skull
Is getting wet.

Death, a skeleton
Neither fat nor skinny.
A homemade skeleton
Stuck together with wax.
—Traditional

CHAPTER EIGHT

FOOD FOR THE DEAD

There are special foods for Día de los Muertos. One is *pan de muerto* (PAHN day MWER-toh). That means "bread of the dead." It's usually a round loaf. The icing on top looks like bones and skulls. A tiny, fake skeleton may be inside.

Another food is *calaveritas* (kah-lah-veh-REE-tahs). Those are skull-shaped candies. They're mostly made of sugar. A dead person's name is on each piece. Both pan de muerto and calaveritas are placed on the altars. They are sweet treats for the dead!

Calaveritas is Spanish for "little skulls."

Pan de muerto and calaveritas are a tasty way to welcome the dead home!

Mexicans have many sayings about death. One is: *La muerte es flaca y no ha de poder conmigo.* That's Spanish for "Death is skinny (or weak) and has no power over me."

Joining in the Spirit of *Día de los Muertos*

- Do you know a Mexican American? Ask him or her about family celebrations for Día de los Muertos.

- Is there a Mexican neighborhood in your community? Find out if it holds a Día de los Muertos festival. If so, go and enjoy the colorful sights!

- Write a poem about funny skeletons. Can you see how skeletons don't have to be scary?

- Find an easy recipe for sugar candy. Have a grown-up help you make it. Shape the candy into little skulls.

Making a *Día de los Muertos*
Vegetable Skeleton

Ingredients:
1 cucumber
1 tomato
1 black olive
1 green pepper or red pepper
2 cups carrot sticks
½ cup low-fat dip or salad dressing

Directions:
Dice the cucumber and tomato into wedges, and slice the olive into smaller rings.* Cutting from the top downward, divide the pepper in half. Place the pepper on a serving platter so that the inside is face down. Arrange the carrot sticks, cucumber, and tomato to create arms, legs, ribs, and other bones. Use a little of the low-fat dip or salad dressing to stick the olive rings to the pepper for eyes, a mouth hole, and a nose hole. Your creation is sure to be a colorful Día de los Muertos offering! Don't forget to celebrate this joyful festival by sampling the various parts of your skeleton with the leftover dip or dressing.

Have an adult help you with the cutting.

Making a Pasta Skeleton

Here's a fun skeleton project that will help get you in the mood for a Día de los Muertos celebration.

What you need:
Uncooked dry pasta in different shapes (wagon wheels, macaroni,
    spirals, spaghetti, etc.)
A piece of black construction paper
Glue
A white crayon

Instructions:
1. Place pasta shapes on the black construction paper to form a skeleton.
    Don't glue them down until you have the skeleton laid out. Be sure it
    looks like you want it to. Also be sure it fits on the paper!
2. Glue the pasta on the paper one piece at a time.
3. Let the glue dry completely.
4. Use the white crayon to write your name or to give your skeleton a
    name.

Place the skeleton on your ofrenda and enjoy the holiday!

Words to Know

altars *(ALL-turz)* tables set up for religious devotion

cycle *(SY-kuhl)* a set of events that keeps repeating

grim *(GRIHM)* gloomy

symbols *(SIM-bulz)* objects that stand for an idea

How to Learn More about Día de los Muertos

At the Library

Luenn, Nancy, and Robert Chapman (illustrator). *A Gift for Abuelita: Celebrating the Day of the Dead.* Flagstaff, Ariz.: Rising Moon, 1998.

Müller, Birte, and Marianne Martens (translator). *Felipa and the Day of the Dead.* New York: North-South Books, 2004.

Orozco, José-Luis, and Elisa Kleven (illustrator). *Fiestas: A Year of Latin American Songs of Celebration.* New York: Dutton Children's Books, 2002.

San Vicente, Luis, and John Byrd and Bobby Byrd (translators). *The Festival of Bones/El Festival de las Calaveras: The Little-Bitty Book for the Day of the Dead.* El Paso, Tex.: Cinco Puntos Press, 2002.

On the Web

Visit our home page for lots of links about Día de los Muertos:
http://www.childsworld.com/links
NOTE TO PARENTS, TEACHERS, AND LIBRARIANS:
We routinely verify our Web links to make sure they're safe, active sites—so encourage your readers to check them out!

ABOUT THE AUTHOR

Ann Heinrichs lives in Chicago, Illinois. She has written more than two hundred books for children. She loves traveling to faraway places.

ABOUT THE ILLUSTRATOR

Mernie Gallagher-Cole has illustrated many books for children. She lives in West Chester, Pennsylvania, with her husband Rick, daughter Glenna, and son Ian.

Index